What's it like to be... an ANT?

Jinny Johnson

illustrated by **Desiderio Sanzi**

W

FRANKLIN WATTS
LONDON • SYDNEY

(A) An Appleseed Editions book

First published in 2013 by Franklin Watts
338 Euston Road, London NW1 3BH

© 2011 Appleseed Editions

Created by Appleseed Editions Ltd,
Well House, Friars Hill, Guestling,
East Sussex TN35 4ET

Designed and illustrated by Guy Callaby
Edited by Mary-Jane Wilkins

ISBN 978 1 4451 2187 1

Dewey Classification: 595.7'96

A CIP catalogue for this book is available
from the British Library.

Printed in China

Franklin Watts is a division of
Hachette Children's Books,
an Hachette UK company.
www.hachette.co.uk

Contents

An ant is an insect.

It has six legs and a pair of feelers on its head.

So what's it like to be an ant?

It's hard work being an ant.

I'm busy all the time.

I live in a nest in the woods with lots of other ants.

Our nest is made of dead leaves, pine needles, twigs and earth.

Inside our nest there are tunnels, rooms and places to store our food.

Our mother is the queen
ant and the head of our family.

She lays all the eggs.

There may
be 100,000 ants
in a nest.

The rest of us look after the
queen and bring her food.

I started life as an egg. It was about the size of a pinhead.

I hatched out into a little squirmy larva.

A larva has no legs, but can wriggle around.

I grew until I was about the size of your little fingernail. Then I spun a silk case around myself.

I turned into a young ant inside my silk case.

When I came out, I was a bit weak and wobbly at first.

Other ants looked after me until I could manage by myself.

Then I started work.

I am a worker ant,
like most ants in our family.

*Worker ants
like me don't have
wings.*

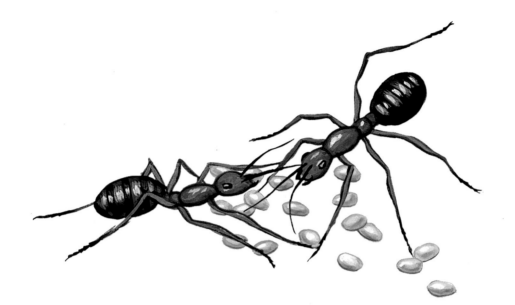

My first job was looking after the eggs and young.

I brought them food and kept them clean.

When I was older I started
to go out with other workers
to find food.

Every day we march off
to look for caterpillars and
other insects to bring back.

*I'm strong. I can carry food that
is three times as heavy as me.*

We leave a smelly trail so other workers can follow us and we don't get lost.

One day I will be a guard ant and protect our nest.

If other insects attack our nest we fight back.

We bite the attackers and spray them with liquid we make in our bodies.

It stings!

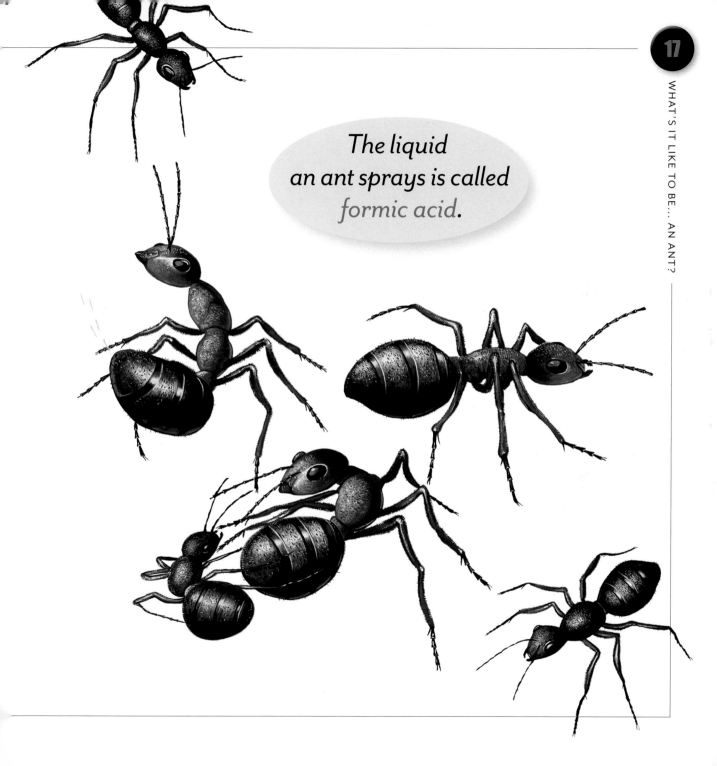

*The liquid
an ant sprays is called
formic acid.*

Not all the eggs our queen lays hatch into workers.

Some hatch into male ants with wings.

Male ants don't do any work and are fed by other ants.

Others hatch into new queens and they have wings too.

One summer day every year
some males and queens
fly out of our nest.

They mate, then the males die.

The queen bites off her wings.
Then she goes back to the nest
to lay eggs, or starts a new nest.

More about ants

What are an ant's feelers for?

An ant uses its feelers, called antennae, to smell and taste what is around it. The ant's eyesight is poor but its feelers are very sensitive. The ant can bend them forward or hold them back out of the way.

Do all ants make nests?

Most do, but not all. Army ants are nearly always on the move so they don't make nests. At night they gather round their queen to protect her.

How many kinds of ants are there?

There may be at least 12,000 different kinds of ants and there are probably lots more we don't know about yet.

What do ants eat?

Most ants eat other insects, including other ants! They also eat fruit and vegetables and the bodies of animals that have died.

Ant words

antennae
A pair of long, thin body parts on an insect's head. Antennae are also known as feelers.

formic acid
Stinging liquid sprayed by some ants to warn off enemies.

larva
A worm-like creature. An ant spends the first part of its life as a larva.

queen ant
The leader of the group. The queen lays all the eggs.

worker ant
An ant that gathers food, looks after young and defends the nest.

Ant index

antennae 22, 23

eggs 6, 7, 8, 13, 20

feelers 3, 22, 23
formic acid 17, 23

guard ants 16, 17

larva 8, 23

male ants 18, 20

nest 4, 5, 7, 16, 20, 22

queen ant 6, 7, 18, 19, 20, 23

worker ants 12, 13, 14, 15, 18, 23

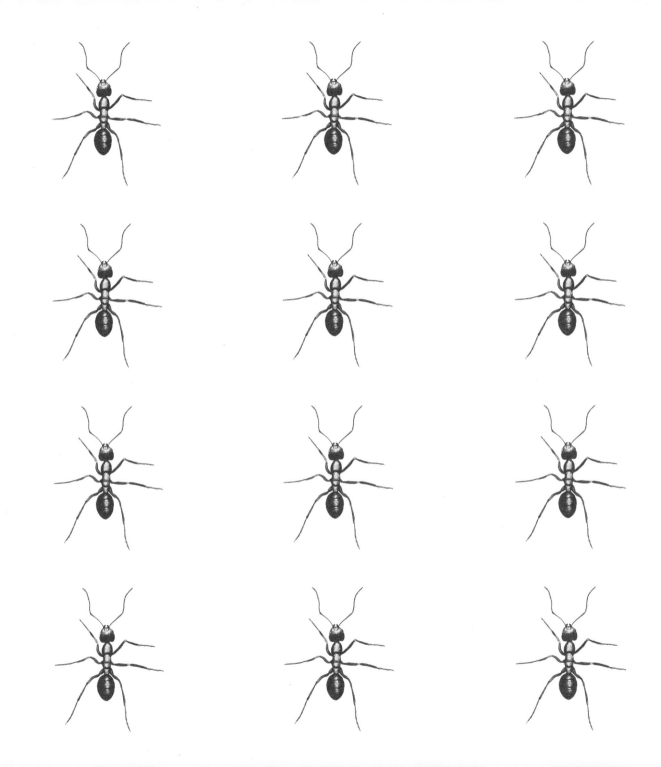